CURB PAINTING

From the

"Little Books of Extra Cash" Series

Volume 1

Eddie Patin

How to Make Extra Income with

Your Own Two Feet and some Paint

Copyright

"Curb Painting" 2nd Edition

"Little Books of Extra Cash"

Copyright © 2016, Lost Woods Publishing LLC

http://LostWoodsPublishing.com

To join Eddie Patin's free mailing list, for updates about new titles:

http://LostWoodsPublishing.com/eddiepatin

EBooks are not transferable. All Rights Are Reserved. No part of this book may be used or reproduced in any manner without written permission, except in the case of brief quotations embodied in critical articles and reviews. The unauthorized reproduction or distribution of this copyrighted work is illegal. No part of this book may be scanned, uploaded, or distributed via the Internet or any other means, electronic or print, without the publisher's permission.

Published in the United States of America by Lost Woods Publishing LLC, 2015

> *"I always think that if you read a book and come away with one or more good ideas, you have received your money's worth. I've gained a couple of different helpful ideas from reading this book. In my opinion, it's worth the purchase!"*
>
> - Lisa, Amazon Reviewer (previous edition)

Need some extra cash?

Curb painting is an easy way to make some extra side income--either as a supplement to your normal income, a little extra to help pay the bills, or even as a full-time job! You are in full control, and can go out TODAY, with a minimal amount of cheap equipment, to make some money immediately.

Learn this simple skill as a side business that you can always use to help make your monthly expenses, tide you over between jobs, save extra money, experiment with ground-level entrepreneurship (as an adult or a teenager!), or just make some extra cash! In this guide, you'll learn about the business of curb painting, the equipment you'll need, details about organizing your business, scripts and advice for dealing with customers, instructions for painting the curb, and much more.

The "*Little Books of Extra Cash*" Series reflects the author's experiences developing an entrepreneureal mindset during the beginning of the latest American recession, when work was hard to come by and he had to apply himself creatively to survive. All of these "Little Books of Extra Cash" will show you ways to make side money 'off the grid', deal in CASH, and be limited only by your own ambition.

Table of Contents

Contents

Author's Preface – 2nd Edition 1

Introduction 7
    Little Books of Extra Cash 7

Chapter 1: What is Curb Painting? 13
    Curb Painting as a Cash Job 13
    Overview of this Guide 20

Chapter 2: The Equipment You'll Need 23
    What You Can Buy 23
    What You Can Make 39
    Extra Equipment to Bring Along 55
    My Equipment Kit 59

Chapter 3: The Business 63
    Your Focus 63
    Plotting Your Course 73
    Facing Your Customers 86

Painting That Curb 110
Recording Your Results 126
What Others Have Done 133

Chapter 4: Summary 147

About the Author – Eddie Patin 159

More Titles from Eddie Patin 161

A Message from Lost Woods Publishing 167

Author's Preface - 2nd Edition

Welcome, new readers. It's 2016. A long walk from when I originally wrote this book in 2009, but the premise is still very real.

If you're looking for a real way to make some extra money, you've come to the right place. There are oodles of books out there by gurus and wealthy experts who are supposedly so flush with cash from their expertise that they want to 'share the knowledge' and make the world a better place. They promise you that if you follow particular steps, you'll be on your way to making millions.

Oh, after you subscribe to their monthly service, of course.

"Curb Painting"

That's not what these 'Little Books of Extra Cash' are about.

If you're looking at this book, it means you're struggling in some way financially. You're either totally broke, or you're working, and maybe getting by, but you're looking for ideas to make things better.

This little book will outline for you how you can go out on your own gumption, if you have a real need for some extra money, and make money out of thin air by your entrepreneurial effort. Eventually, I'll have a whole series of "Little Books of Extra Cash", but it all started with this one. This is a foundation. Something you can do, a tool in your repertoire, to go out and make some cash when you need to.

"Curb Painting"

Curb painting won't make you a millionaire, obviously. But it's a very real 'boots on the ground' idea to make some extra income when you need it.

Maybe you're a grown adult down on your luck, and need to make some money to start something else. Or a little extra to pay your cellphone bill. Or, perhaps, as a working stiff, you're just looking to build up and save some extra money in your time off. Or maybe you're a teenager trying to sink your teeth into earning your own money for the first time, and want to be more creative than just working at a fast food joint.

No matter *why* you're here, reading about ideas to make side cash, since you have this book, read on, and you'll be endowed with an idea—a skill—that you'll always have for the rest of your

"Curb Painting"

life. You'll have your curb painting 'bucket kit'. I can tell you, I still have mine.

So, since 2009, life has gone on. The economy is still shaky. Not necessarily better or worse, but in the last few years, I've gotten the feeling that people are a little more relaxed as a whole about spending their money. You should still be able to wrangle up an average of $15-25 an hour doing this, and you can still buy all of the basic equipment super cheaply at Wal-Mart, etc.

Technology is better. When I walked the suburbs painting numbers on curbs in 2008 & 2009, I used a physical map book. Now, you can just use your phone and a map app. I would still probably use a paper map, however, because it's easier to mark and plan your route. But everyone has a phone with Google Maps and GPS now.

The business plan isn't very different.

The idea of going out into the world with a particular skill and service to offer people is timeless. If you have something of value that helps others, you can always offer to perform that service in exchange for pay. It's as old as currency.

So read on, and learn another skill. A simple skill. Something that you can use to get up off of your butt and go pocket some cash *today* if you want to.

Enjoy this 'Little Book of Extra Cash', and please make sure to leave a review on Amazon when you're done. Those Amazon reviews go a long way.

- *Eddie Patin, 2016*

"Curb Painting"

Introduction

Little Books of Extra Cash

Welcome to the Little Books of Extra Cash series!

These are tough times we're living in. At the time when I am writing these series of books, we (in the United States) have been delving into a recession. People have been losing their jobs. Worse yet, people that don't *have* a job, and trying to *find* a job, have been discovering the once-easy job market nearly *impossible* to breach.

Have you been out there pounding the pavement? Or sitting at home, your vision blurred from scanning ad to ad on *Craigslist* or *Monster.com*? If you have, you've probably been feeling the squeeze and the hopelessness when every other ad out there is a work-from-home scam, and any real, legitimate job listings ... are being flooded with two hundred resumes *a day*.

Even highly experienced professionals, with incredible resumes, are being lost in a swamp of desperate applicants.

I began this little series of books throughout my own difficulties finding work in an economy that is degrading a little more every day, so that I could share with you all the various ways I have been getting by. These are creative ways I've used my experience, and a little entrepreneurial spirit, to come up with extra cash to pay the bills.

"Curb Painting"

Make no mistake—absolutely NONE of these 'little books of extra cash' will make you 'rich'. But they will *help*. And if you are finding it impossible to get a job—even a job waving a sign on the corner—these little books will show you ways to work, on your own, to come up with the money you need to get by.

Most of these 'side jobs' you could do full-time, if you were so inclined, and you'd have the satisfaction of working for yourself, without having to rely upon an employer. Also, you'll always have a skill to fall back on whenever you come across hard times. And if you *are* currently working, you'll find that these self-generated jobs can always be performed during the weekend, evenings, etc., in case you'd just like to make some extra income.

"Curb Painting"

These are 'cash jobs'. Work where you mainly deal in cash. No paychecks. Being able to head out in the morning to 'make money' on your own steam, and come home later that day or in the evening with a pocket full of cash—that's far more valuable than having to wait on a bi-monthly paycheck.

Each of these jobs, in this series, I have performed myself. I have either come up with the idea on my own, strategized, worked the job, and refined the job until it was as efficient as possible, *or*, I have seen others do the job, and got involved myself to the point where I could do it successfully on my own. Each job, once perfected, will be passed on to you.

So ... need some extra cash?

"Curb Painting"

Well, I want to thank you for purchasing this 'little book of extra cash'. It is a 'little book'. You won't find any 'filler' here—I want you to be able to get started as soon as possible. So read on, learn the basics, get your supplies … and get to work!

"Curb Painting"

Chapter 1: What is Curb Painting?

Curb Painting as a Cash Job

When you drive around in your neighborhood—or any neighborhood—have you ever noticed the black and white address numbers out on the sidewalk near peoples' driveways?

Most neighborhoods in America, young and old, have address numbers painted out on the curb.

But how do those numbers get there?

Curb painters.

"Curb Painting"

A very small minority of people paint the curb numbers for their own houses, because they'd have to buy a set of stencils that they'd likely use for only that single purpose. Since painted numbers are only touched up once every one or two years, most people would not consider buying the stencils, and storing them somewhere in their garage, worth the trouble.

There are a few people out there, hardly noticeable, going door to door and painting, or touching up, these curb numbers.

I originally came up with the idea of curb painting (for myself—the idea did already exist, of course) one January while I was between jobs and brainstorming for extra work ideas. When I was a teenager, I remember my father once telling me about a neighbor's boy who was running a small business for himself painting address numbers on the sidewalk. Back then, I was only concerned with playing computer games and listening to *Offspring*, so I didn't think much of it. That neighbor boy has since become a successful entrepreneur. He probably doesn't paint curbs anymore, but it was a good kick-start to a more independent and entrepreneurial state of mind.

Considering the idea again as a 'small business', my research pulled up *very little* in the way of guides, documents, books—not a single website specialized on the subject. The only places I found any reference to curb-painting was the off-hand mention of the business as a project for Boy Scout Troops, and the more involved business of painting entire curbs (i.e. 'no parking' red zones, etc.) or parking space lines.

"Curb Painting"

Cash jobs are best when you can think of something that is very cheap (it needs to be ultra-cheap if you're going door-to-door), has high demand, and doesn't have much competition. As far as a cash job went, I found that the variables involved in curb painting were very ideal:

Curb painting, as a product and service:

- Is very cheap. The rate is very reasonable for just about *any* customer, and it's pretty hard for the average customer to turn you down—unless they're cheap, very frugal, or do it themselves.

- Is a renewable service. The paint on the curb wears off. It's scuffed up by tires and it's stained by rain.

- Has an unlimited market. It can be done anywhere. I don't know how things are in other countries, but here (in America), nearly *all* neighborhoods have address numbers painted on the curb, rich or poor. There are the *very* seldom neighborhoods that have HOA (Home Owners' Association) rules against it, but I've found that even in those taboo neighborhoods, many homeowners don't know … or don't care. If you find a virgin neighborhood with no paint, well, it's going to be painted sooner or later. The curb painter may as well be you.

- Has a very good income-per-job to time-spent-per-job ratio. I'll get into time, volume, and rates later on.

"Curb Painting"

- Has virtually *no* overhead or expenses. Once you get your (pretty cheap) initial kit set up, you're only spending money on gas and paint.

- You can do the job anytime. As long as it isn't raining, or sporting a foot of snow. In fact, if you don't mind carrying some more equipment, you can even work when there's snow in the gutters (if you *really, really* want to).

Curb painting became a major staple of on-the-side cash work for me. I've found that getting a job isn't the same anymore as it was before, say, 2007. It takes a lot of time and patience to find anything (above minimum wage)—especially something permanent. Today, when a company or staffing agency puts out a job ad, that company is being

"Curb Painting"

flooded with *hundreds* of resumes, making standing out among the masses a ridiculous affair, and extremely unlikely that they'll get around to you or me. Even jobs so easy to obtain before 'the crunch' are hard to come by, especially if you're young, because so many over-qualified people will over-shadow the folks that don't have twenty years of experience.

Whatever troubles you may be having in the job market, or if you simply want some extra cash, curb painting is an easy way to make a moderate income if you have the desire to get out there and work. For $20 or so in materials, if you go at it bare-bones, you can make $15 to $20 dollars an hour or more. And it's *your* schedule—so it's really up to you.

"Curb Painting"

Overview of this Guide

Once we get into the next chapter, we'll start assembling the nuts and bolts of this simple, little side-business.

We'll begin with the equipment you need, which isn't much. With just the bare-minimum essentials, you can hack out that extra income you need. Of course, you can get as elaborate as you like, if you want to do a better, or quicker, job, or use more professional equipment—but you don't need to. It's all up to you. No matter how much you want to invest in your 'kit', remember: it's only curb painting. If you purchase *everything*, including the optional stuff, you won't go over fifty bucks.

I'll show you what equipment you have to buy, and why. The necessary and the optional. I'll also show you what to make yourself, and talk about any extra gear you might want to bring along. Lastly, I'll tell you what's in my personal curb painting kit.

Once you have your kit together, we'll talk about the business itself. This is the meat of it—all the stuff I had to figure out on the fly. While there are plenty of details in this wee business (but it's no sweat—really), I'll point out the important stuff you should be focusing on. What really matters to you and your income.

We'll talk about how to get out there, get started, and how to plot your course. After that, I'll go over the part that may be the scariest for most of you—facing the customers. What to say, how to say it. And don't worry. I'll include plenty of scripts

"Curb Painting"

for you to follow. We'll talk a little about the nature of working in a door-to-door environment.

Then I'll show you how to paint a curb. Quickly and easily. And how to do a good job while you're at it.

At the end of the 'Business' section, I'll go over how and why to record your results, what to *do* with those records, and a few more ideas to expand the business, if you choose.

So kick back, turn the page, and learn a trade.

Chapter 2: The Equipment You'll Need

What You Can Buy

Every business of any size requires an initial investment of some sort, even something as small as curb painting. You can spend between $20 (for the minimum) up to about $50 if you want to include all the optional equipment, but for this little cash job, you should never have to invest any more than that.

When I got started with curb painting, I was able to find *most* of the things I needed at Wal-Mart. The Stencils were harder to find, which I eventually located at Lowes, but you should also be

"Curb Painting"

able to find them at Home Depot or any other hardware store.

So let's get started:

A Bucket / Pail - $2 - $10

You'll be on your feet when you're curb painting, and you'll need something in which to carry around all of your gear. You've got to be able to carry several cans of spray paint, a bottle of water, and various other doodads, so, I've found that a bucket is the best way to go. Remember that you'll be carrying that bucket around for hours in one hand, so it has to have some sort of 'hand relief' on the handle (as opposed to a plain metal-wire handle). Most modern buckets have these anyway, at least in the form of a rotating plastic dowel.

I bought my (first) bucket from Wal-Mart—the cheapest, most basic bucket I could find. It was round, plastic, and blue, and sold for $1.24. Later, I *upgraded* to a square-shaped bucket (more like $6), because it was better for holding the cans of spray-paint.

Gloves - $2 or more

Any sort of work gloves will be needed, unless you want to get paint on your hands. I bought some cheap 'jersey' gloves for $1.94 from Wal-Mart. When I'm actually out there, though, I only wear *one* of them. I keep one hand free for manipulating money and being able to access my

"Curb Painting"

pocket, and the other hand is gloved for holding the stencils down when I'm painting.

Spray Paint - $1 - $5 each

You'll want to pick up several of these. At a minimum, you'll want to start with *two* cans of black, and *three* cans of white (you'll use more white than black). Then, once you make some cash, you can go back to the store and buy some more.

Now, a big debate about curb painting is about whether to use the basic, *dollar* spray paint, or to use the fancy reflective spray paint for designed for concrete. I've always used the basic, cheap 96-cent spray paint from Wal-Mart, because *all* paint, fancy or not, will eventually wear off and need touching up anyway. Then, later, you can go back and touch it up yourself. Also, the reflective paint is nice, but I just don't find it strong enough as a selling point to potential customers to offset the high price. Remember that paint is your biggest expense, and reflective paint will seriously cut into your profits.

If you have enough money in the beginning, make sure to stock up on paint. You can always leave the extras in your car, and switch them out as necessary.

A City Map - $5 - $20

This is something I would personally consider a necessity, but, depending on the size of and your familiarity with your town, you can skip it if you like. A map is an important tool, however, for maximizing your efficiency. Spending more time on

"Curb Painting"

foot and less time moving from spot to spot in your car. It will also let you keep track of where you've been, and assist you in recording your progress, taking notes, and planning future curb painting strategies.

A basic, fold-up map of your city can be obtained from Wal-Mart or other stores for around five bucks. I prefer one of the map *books*, though. In my city, I use a Randy McNally spiral-bound map book, purchased for $20 (at Wal-Mart).

Highlighter(s) - $1 - $2 each

If you buy a map, buy a highlighter for marking your progress.

Notebook and Pen(s)/Pencil(s) - $3 - $5 for both

If you want to maximize your efficiency (i.e., make more money for time spent), figure out how much cash you're pulling in per hour, remember which neighborhoods are better than others, etc., you'll have to *write things down*. Purchase a notebook of some sort to record your progress. Make sure the notebook is tough enough to resist being rattled around in your bucket and small enough to avoid wasting space.

Cheap Dustpan - $1 at Wal-Mart

I originally bought a cheap, plastic dustpan (97 cents from Wal-Mart) with the idea of using it as a paint shield to make my white edges. *That* didn't work out so well. However, the dustpan *did* prove

"Curb Painting"

very useful as a *fan*, and I always carry it around with me. As you'll see later in the book, the curb painting takes place in two painting stages: the white background, then the black numbers. If you have a dustpan, you can fan the fresh white paint to help it dry faster, and you won't have to wait as long to get to the black paint. This will make the job *faster*, leaving you more time to hit the road and do more jobs.

You could consider a dustpan as optional equipment, but it's worked well for me, and it's only a buck.

4-inch Stencils - $6 or more

This might be the hardest piece of equipment for you to find. When I first got into curb painting, I had to call around to various hard-ware stores to find them, and to make sure the stencils they actually *had* in stock were the right style and size.

> (2nd *Edition Side Note – As of 2016, a set of 4" or 5" re-useable stencils are easily obtainable from Amazon.*)

I eventually found a set of 4-inch, re-usable stencils. They were water-resistant, made of a thick stencil board, and of the *standard universal* style. The pack I bought was $5.66 at Lowes, and came with letters and numbers (you'll only need the numbers).

Here is a link to the same product on Lowes' website:

"Curb Painting"

http://www.lowes.com/pd_236782-37672-839726_1z0ykaw_?productId=3054385&pl=1

The important thing to consider in a stencil set is the *size* and the *style*. There are many sizes available. The vast majority of curb numbers are painted with *four inch* stencils. Also, before you go shopping, take a good look at some real curb numbers on the way to the store. Note the style. You'd have no trouble finding stencils if you didn't care about the 'font' or style—they've got plenty of foofy or swoopy fonts at Wal-Mart and hobby stores. But make sure you stick with that 'universal', plain *block-style* so that your numbers look like everyone else's. If you deviate, you might have some angry customers.

The stencils I mentioned above are *basic* stencils. Cheap. There are also stencils out there that are more specialized for curb painting, such as plastic stencils that lock together for easier painting, etc.—but good luck finding those without special ordering them or searching the Internet for hours.

In fact, in the end, I ended up not using the stencils I bought. I did at first, but they had their drawbacks. Instead, I used those stencils to make some better stencils, which I use today. I'll show you how to make custom stencils like mine a little later.

Poster Board - Less than a dollar

Buy one or two sheets of normal, plain white poster board. You'll use this poster board to make the template for your white background, and it will act as your paint shield, to insure you don't overspray or make messy edges.

Wire Brush - $5 or more new, less used

This is an optional piece of equipment. They vary in price, but you can get a used one from a garage sale or thrift store if you like. A plain old wire brush can be used for two things:

1. To brush off the surface of the old numbers, or wherever the new numbers will be going, to make sure the surface is (relatively) clean and will allow the paint to stick properly.

2. To clear out the gutter. If the gutter is full of muck and plant junk, that garbage will get

"Curb Painting"

in the way of your paint shield and make it harder to do a good job.

I say that the wire brush is optional, because I've never needed one. I've always just wiped off the surface I'm about to paint with my glove, or displaced the dirt and dust with a wave of the dustpan fan. If the gutter is ever full of debris, I'll either clear it out with my heel before sitting down, or find a stick or something to use as a quick tool.

Putty Knife - $5 or more new, less used

Another optional piece of equipment. When you paint over your stencils, you've got to use something to hold the stencil down against the concrete so that you have no gapping and good edges. I've seen some curb painters use a putty

"Curb Painting"

knife for this. Instead, I've always just used my gloved hand, careful to minimize how much paint I get on my glove.

Something to Sit or Kneel On - Price Varies

When you're out there curb painting, you'll be walking a lot, knocking on doors, briefly talking to people, and (hopefully) three to four times an hour or more, sitting down on the street or in the gutter to paint some numbers. If you don't have something to sit on, the seat of your pants will get pretty dirty. If you're just wearing 'work pants' like I do, that won't be a big deal. The *big deal*, however, will come when you have to sit down on a moist, damp, or even *wet* street. You'll also see all sorts of rotting vegetation junk accumulating in areas of gutters under trees, or areas full of sand

"Curb Painting"

and mud. Having wet or dirty pants will make walking around for a few hours more difficult—it's definitely annoying for me.

Consider something small (that will fit in your bucket) to sit on. Padded or not, its most important purpose should be to keep you from getting wet.

In most 'gardening departments', you'll be able to find a basic, little foam rectangle, with a hole cut into one side for a handle. That would be swell. If you've ever spent time on your knees pulling weeds in a garden, you probably know *exactly* the piece of equipment I'm talking about. You can be more creative though, and even find something cheaper. I, myself, carry around a large, laminated placemat that came from the kitchen section of Wal-Mart. It's got our nation's presidents on one side and a map of America on the other. This

"Curb Painting"

placemat keeps my pants dry, rolls up nice and easy to fit in the bucket without being in the way of other gear, and doesn't weigh a thing.

Painting Mask - $1 or so for a multi-pack

If you're ever curb painting in breezy conditions, or prone to getting head-aches from paint fumes, using one of these masks can make the difference between whistling while you work (well—*not really* if you're wearing a mask) and barely being able to tolerate a long, miserable day.

On a normal day, when I paint curbs, I don't even notice the paint fumes. When you're painting into the wind, though, getting paint mist in the face, or breathing it for a length of time, can result in a pretty lousy experience. I usually carry a few of these around with me just in case it turns out that I'd need one. Some people might say that you should wear one of these masks *all the time* while painting. I'll leave that up to you—it's pretty hard to interact with customers while wearing a mask, and a real pain to put the mask on, take the mask off, put the mask on, take the mask off...

If you start getting a headache from paint fumes, just take a small break, make sure you're drinking plenty of water, and wear a mask for a while as you continue painting. You can also keep a mask on all the time, since it's connected to you with an elastic string, and just rotate it around to the back of your neck while you're going door to door.

What You Can Make

"Curb Painting"

There are a few minor 'craft' projects you can undertake to make your equipment better. In the case of the paint shield, you'll *have* to make one, because you can't buy a paint shield, specific to curb painting, anywhere I've found.

The Paint Shield

What you'll need:
- One white poster board
- A pencil
- A ruler or straight edge
- Scissors
- Duct tape

The poster board you bought earlier will be used to make a 'template' for the white background that goes behind the address numbers. This will define the white rectangle that ends up on the sidewalk, and act to prevent over-spraying in all four directions on all sides. When you're finished, it will look like a large rectangle, with a rectangular hole cut out of the middle of it.

One sheet of poster board can create two paint shields, and have a little poster board left over. We'll make the paint shield strong, and reinforce it to last a while, but they *are* expendable. They'll eventually soften up, tear in the corners, or be torn in a strong gust of wind. You'll make more as you need them, whenever the one you're painting with is used up or otherwise destroyed. In fact, it's a good idea to keep a backup paint shield in your car when you're out there, or at least the raw materials so you can make one on the fly if you need to.

"Curb Painting"

The paint shield will be as wide as the entire *width* of the poster board (the short side), and 12 inches tall. Please refer to the diagrams while following the directions.

Step one:

Measure 12 inches up from the bottom (or top) of the poster board and mark off both sides. Make sure you're measuring along the *long* side of the board. Make your line accurately (with a long straight edge, or with careful folding, or with more measurements throughout the middle) to define your cut. Make your cut. You should now have a piece of poster board that measure 12 inches tall by 22 inches wide.

Step Two:

Now you'll make your measurements for the rectangular 'window' inside your piece of poster board. When you use this in the field, this window will become the white background for the address numbers. Measure and mark 3 inches into the poster board from each side. Once you've made your markings, you can use your straight edge to make the lines that will show the inner rectangle.

Step Three:

Carefully cut out the inner rectangle. You might find it easiest to use the scissors and poke a hole on the center of the piece of poster board (this is an area you'll throw away), and work to your lines

"Curb Painting"

from there. Be very careful around the corners to keep them crisp and intact. Once you're finished, you'll have a big rectangular 'ring', 3 inches wide all around.

Step Four:

Use duct tape to reinforce all corners on the paint shield's inner window. The poster board will become soft and delicate at its inner edges once it gets wet with paint from several jobs. Taping the corners will help it resist tearing. Don't just tape diagonally *through* the corners, either. That will round them. Tape vertically and horizontally on each corner, right up to the adjacent edge. If this is hard to understand, take a look at the diagram.

"Curb Painting"

Step Five:

Decide which long side of your shield will be the *bottom*. We'll be putting a crease there, to bend the shield at a 90 degree angle, which will make painting a vertical curb a piece of cake. Measure up from the bottom edge 2 1/2 inches in multiple positions and create a clean line. Carefully (start by pinching in multiple, staggered places) fold the poster board over that line—carefully, so you have a very accurate fold. You'll know your fold is in the right place if the inner window has about 1/2 inch of space between the bottom of the window and the fold. This *folded section* will now be the *floor* of the paint shield. It won't make any difference when you have to paint a sloping curb, but for a vertical curb, this folded-over section will simply line up on the ground and be in position automatically.

"Curb Painting"

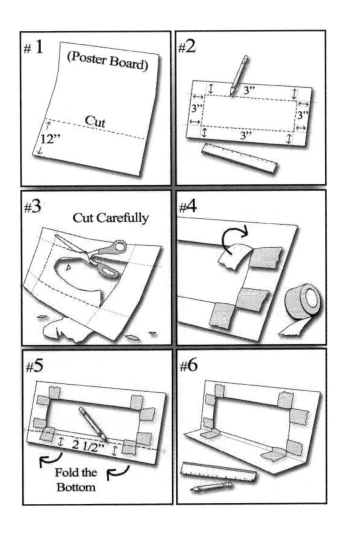

Optional Creation:

Better, Homemade Stencils

As soon as I started painting curbs with the standard stencils I bought from Lowes, I quickly started brainstorming about better stencil ideas. The reason for this is that the four-inch stencils were *okay*, but they're only six inches tall and four inches wide. This is a problem because, while painting over the stencils individually, it was far too easy to over-spray over the edges of the stencil, splattering black on my fresh white paint, and making ugly curb numbers. And if it was a little windy? Forget about it! In breezy conditions, there was no way to avoid 'coloring outside of the lines', and the resulting curb number wasn't nearly as crisp and clean as it should have been.

"Curb Painting"

Standard stencils were also messy to handle, since they were so small, and not very quick to organize, since they'd float around at the bottom of the bucket, or, at best, in a zip-lock bag.

After tossing ideas around for a while, I came up with a better stencil idea that solved these problems: my new stencils were cleaner to handle, eliminated over-spray around the edges, and were easier to keep organized in the bucket. And they were cheap.

What you'll need:
- A razor or box-cutter for precise cutting
- A Sharpie, or other permanent marker
- Translucent, multicolor plastic folder dividers
- Your already-bought (or borrowed) 4 inch Stencils

"Curb Painting"

- A steady hand

It took me some time to find just the right kind of material to make the stencils. I needed something large enough (roughly 8x10 size), made of plastic that was soft enough to be flexible, but tough enough to last. And cheap, of course.

What I eventually found was a packet of 'index tab' folder dividers from Wal-Mart. The dividers came in multiple colors, which became quite handy later, making it easier to quickly choose the number I wanted by remembering the number's *color*. These were the thicker, *matte* dividers—not the 'clearish' glossy ones. I had to buy either two or three packets to have what I needed, since they came five to a pack. The slight translucency came in handy later as well, because I could see the numbers I had already painted *through* the divider,

"Curb Painting"

making it easier to have consistent spacing. Don't get any dividers with built-in pockets, or anything fancy. You're really just looking for a solid sheet of thick plastic.

Okay. So you have the right dividers, and the rest of the supplies you need. Here's what to do, for each number:

Step One:

Take your stencil and lay it on top of one divider, as if you're preparing to paint the number *onto* the divider. Line the stencil up at the *bottom* of the divider, centered horizontally.

"Curb Painting"

Step Two:

Holding the stencil firmly in place, use your marker and trace the number (slowly and accurately!) onto the divider. Next, with the stencil still held firmly in place, trace around the *outside* edge of the stencil onto the divider. This will make a marker 'rectangle' around the number you just drew.

This rectangle of marker you just made will be very useful when you're painting numbers. Since your new stencils will be very large (bigger than 4x6), the *box* you drew will let you line the numbers up with each other, since you can see through the new *semi-transparent* divider stencil. You'll see what I mean when you try it.

"Curb Painting"

Step Three:

Make sure you have something firm under the divider that you don't mind cutting up. Using your razor, *carefully* cut along number you traced in marker. Really take your time here and move *slowly* and *deliberately*. It will take patience and focus to make perfectly straight lines that don't have any rough edges. If you do it right, the numbers on your new stencils will be just as crisp as your old ones—as if cut by a machine.

Step Four:

Using your marker, label each top corner of the new 'divider stencil' with the number *on* the stencil. For instance, if you just made your stencil for number "3", draw two big "3's" in the upper

"Curb Painting"

corners of the stencil. This way, when you're out dong the job, you don't have to pull all the stencils out to find the numbers you need. Just rifle through the corners until you find the right number.

"Curb Painting"

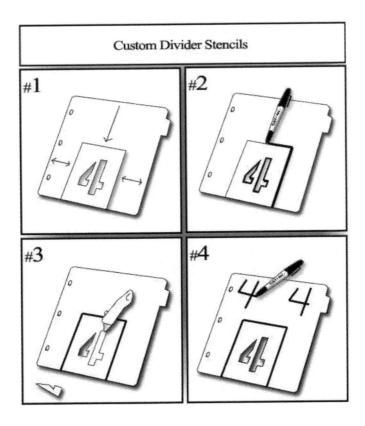

Extra Equipment to Bring Along

So you've got your kit together. What else might you need?

Well, have you ever worked outside for extended periods of time before? What about working in a door-to-door environment? You'll have to be prepared for whatever weather you're *expecting*, be a little prepared for weather you're *not* expecting, make sure you don't look like a *total* bum, and be ready to eat and drink when you need to.

This work is definitely more physical than a desk job. Depending on how long you're planning to work, you could walk for miles over the course of hours. Wear the right shoes. I wear an old pair of gym shoes. That way, they're good and

"Curb Painting"

comfortable for long periods of walking, and I *also* don't care about getting paint on them. (I used my feet to hold the paint shield in place, and I don't care about spraying the side of the shoe soles if it makes my job *faster*.)

Dress as comfortably as you can for walking around all day in the sun. Shorts and a (clean) t-shirt or polo shirt in warm weather. Make sure you're not dressed in rags. You don't have to wear business-casual or anything (*that* would be silly), but you do have to look *moderately* respectable to be taken seriously at the door. I usually wear 'volunteer' t-shirts from various events I've been a part of in the past. Maybe it helps with the sale—maybe not.

Make sure you have a light jacket in the car, or another layer of clothing in case it turns a bit chilly.

If you'll be working in colder weather, adjust accordingly. Just be prepared for *anything*, or your day can be cut short.

You may want to bring a few snacks along, or pack a lunch, which you'll leave in the car. Be prepared to take a lunch if you're working enough hours, just like any normal job. Keep snacks available to munch on whenever you get hungry or feel low on energy. Walking around neighborhoods like this can burn up a *lot* of calories. I also like to keep a few hard candies (like Jolly Ranchers) on hand in case I overheat and the blood sugar gets too low. And, speaking of over-heating:

Water.

Bring water. Drink water. It's easy and convenient to carry around a water-bottle in your

"Curb Painting"

bucket, and refill it as necessary from a gallon jug in your car. Sometimes, I also wear a small *Camelback* backpack, in which I'll also keep extra clothing and supplies, which is nice because the water stays cool and I can carry more, *but*, carrying a backpack for hours will take its own extra toll. If you look forward to the extra exercise, go for it.

I'd advise wearing a hat in hot weather. One that still looks half-way professional. Besides the frequent drinking of water, a hat is a very powerful defense against over-heating, burning, or getting sun-stroke. You should also consider sunscreen.

Another thing to think about that I once learned the hard way: *when* will you be curb painting? What time of the day? If you're trying to get more people when they're home by hitting the streets in the evening, make sure to bring a head-lamp for lighting up your work. Otherwise, once darkness falls, you're done for the day.

My Equipment Kit

My current kit has been assembled, modified, refined, and re-arranged from constant improvements and experience. I could always add more (I don't have all of the optional equipment), but what I have works for me.

What I carry with me:

- A small white, plastic bucket, rectangular-shaped to make arranging the stuff inside easier. (*Wal-Mart*)

"Curb Painting"

- A laminated placemat for sitting on (*Wal-Mart*)
- A *Koller-Craft* 11 inch 'Floor Hugger' Dustpan (*Wal-Mart*)
- Jersey-knit gloves (only the left one) (*Wal-Mart*)
- My custom-made 'Divider Stencils' (*Wal-Mart*)
- Two cans of 'el cheapo' *ColorPlace* fast drying spray paint, black (*Wal-Mart*)
- Three cans of 'el cheapo' *ColorPlace* fast drying spray paint, white (*Wal-Mart*)
- One painter's mask (*Wal-Mart*)
- A map book, or a pre-printed 'google map' of the area I'm visiting, protected by a clear-plastic paper-protector sheath (*Wal-Mart*)
- An old water bottle
- $15 dollars worth of change, in fives, to start with (if I bother)

"Curb Painting"

- My custom-made paint shield
- Maybe a power-bar
- A watch (for timing results)
- A cell phone (worth mentioning)
- An LED head-lamp (if I'm planning on doing work in the dark)

What I keep in the car, or maybe in a backpack:

- A light jacket
- Several more cans of paint in both colors
- My original *Lowes* stencils, for backup
- The package of remaining painter's masks
- A mini-roll of duct tape for fixing tears in the paint shield
- A notebook with pens and/or a pencil for recording results
- Food

"Curb Painting"

- A gallon jug of water
- A poncho (in a backpack only)

So that's all I have to say about equipment. As you can see, you can get started extremely cheaply, if you need to, and get more when you make the money. In fact, I bought minimal paint when I started, then went out and bought more cans on my lunch break. Even fully decked out for this little cash job as I am, I probably wouldn't value my collection of gear at over $40-$50.

Now that the 'stuff' is out of the way, let's move on to the actual business...

Chapter 3: The Business

Your Focus

Curb Painting is a pretty simple job. It's a pretty simple business, too. But as a businessman, even though it's a simple one, you'll have to know where your focus should be.

Just a quick word about business. The fact that you are here, reading this book, tells me that you are either an entrepreneur of some sort, and are no stranger to the business mind, or you're getting the feeling that being an employee is *not* the way to go, and are exploring more options. In case you're in new territory here, you might want to consider reading a book by Robert Kiyosaki, called

"Curb Painting"

'The Cashflow Quadrant'. That book will help bring you into a whole new world of understanding about how you make money in your life, and the mindsets involved.

If you were doing this curb-painting job as an *employee*, working for someone else, there's a ton of stuff you could be focusing on—conversations with customers, annoying customers, being annoyed with how many people aren't home, or how many people are renting, or details about the painting, or driving, or planning, etc.

As a business owner working for yourself, all of these things are secondary. The real focus, the thing you adjust everything else to adapt to ... is the bottom line. The profit going into your pocket. *All* you have to focus on is getting that *volume*, and trying to keep your income *per hour* as high as possible.

Volume

In this business, focus on keeping your volume as high as possible. That means constantly asking yourself the question, "How could I be getting in front of *more* potential customers in *less* time?" Individually, you'll have lots of people saying 'no', a few people that refuse to even talk to you, a few people that *can't* talk to you over the obnoxious yipping of their poodles, and lots of people that aren't home. But occasionally, you'll have one person that says, "Sure, okay," and hands you five bucks. And far more often, you'll have a person who initially says no, but then says, "Well ... okay," after you give them a quick 'rebuttal'.

"Curb Painting"

How many doors can you knock on in one hour? And how many people will open those doors and talk to you? If only three people buy your little curb painting service in an hour, you've made $15 that hour, which is a pretty good hourly rate for making money out of thin air.

If you get bogged down in the details, all those *no's* and 'not home's are just going to make you angry, bump up the stress, and burn you out. I'll get more into the specific mindset of working door-to-door in a little while, but just remember: it's all about the *volume*. Think of it like a numbers game. If it takes ten *no's* to get a *yes*, then the faster you move and the less down-time you suffer, the more *no's* you can get through until you finally get to that *yes*. And the more doors you knock on, the higher the volume, the more *yes*'s you'll earn.

"Curb Painting"

Charging five bucks a pop, even two jobs will get you an hourly rate of $10 (more than day-labor), and only two *yes's* an hour will sure seem far and in between over that hour's time.

That point there is that just two *yes*'s an hour will feel like an eternity of rejection, but will *still* net you a competitive $10 an hour.

You'd have to be rather unlucky, or have something *off* about you (driving people away) to get less than an average of three jobs an hour. And there will be hours where you get job after job, or even jobs where people pay to have their curb *and their neighbor's curb* touched up.

So when you're out there, and you're stressing out because of a bad run of rejection, just focus on the volume. The volume will get you through it, and the volume will make you money.

Also, as I'll discuss later, the more efficient you can get your routes (more time on your feet and less time in your car, less breaks, etc.), the more money you can make. The more doors you can knock on in an hour, the more you move the numbers in your favor, and the more you can *statistically* earn in an hour.

Your volume will directly affect your income per hour.

At the rate you're charging for your services, it'll be really easy to calculate your hourly rate. As I'll discuss in the 'keeping records' section, you'll want to keep an eye on the clock as you walk the neighborhoods. Keeping *volume* in mind, an hour

"Curb Painting"

will go by pretty quickly when you set a goal for yourself (say—three jobs an hour for an income of $15 per hour). And as time goes by, closing in on the end of your current hour, you'll be thinking to yourself,

> "I'm doing great. One more in twenty minutes, and I'll make the $15 for the hour,"

... or,

> "I've done five jobs in thirty-five minutes! Let's see how many more I can do in the rest of the hour!"

... or,

"Curb Painting"

> "Man, what a slow hour. I've only got fifteen minutes to get two more jobs—I'd better step up the game."

Don't focus on the whole—focus on small parts. Instead of thinking of how much you'll make over the entire day, take it in small chunks. Hour to hour. By focusing on keeping your volume high, and figuring out the *rate* you earned each hour that goes by, the money will come, and you'll be pleasantly surprised at the end of the day to add it all up, figure your averages, and see that you were making, say, $17.25 an hour. Or $22.50 an hour. Or $13.00 an hour on a really slow day.

One last thing about your focus:

You'll be doing great by just focusing on the volume and achieving a particular hourly rate.

While you're out there, though, make sure you're *doing a good job*.

If you've only worked as someone else's employee all your life, you'll be pretty jazzed, especially in the beginning, when you're out there putting cash in your pocket, earned on your own steam. On days when you'll be doing really well, you'll even have a grin plastered on your face, which, of course, will also increase the effectiveness of your sales and make you do even better.

With all this focus on the business aspect of curb painting, though, and avoiding getting bogged down in the details, remember that you're *performing a service for pay*. Make sure you do the job, as small as it is, to the *best* of your ability. Take pride in your work.

"Curb Painting"

Offering a service, doing a great job, and being proud of the job you did and the income it earned, is a cornerstone of Capitalism, and part of what makes this country great. When you do a job and are paid directly for your results, you'll have much more of a connection with the economy, the job market, and your own personal self-worth. You'll feel like a provider—you were paid directly for something you did. Something you created. And you'll say to yourself, "What crummy economy?"

Likewise, when you're working for a convenience store, or waiting tables, or any number of meaningless jobs, you'll grumble when you have to perform a task. Don't grumble here. Remember that you're out there, walking the sidewalks, by your own choice. You're making money by your own gumption, for better or for worse, and you have a small trade that will earn bread on the table, instead of sitting around at home. If you're grumbling when you're out there, fed up and doing lousy work, you may as well stay home.

But you're here, reading this, so that tells me that you're at least a little curious about taking the bull by the horns and making money for yourself—your way. So, let's move on to plotting your course.

Plotting Your Course

This market is everywhere. *Everywhere.* I was surprised to see these address numbers in every neighborhood, big and small, rich or poor, which I had never really noticed before I started looking for them. In *any* city or town, where there are

"Curb Painting"

sidewalks in front of houses, there *are* or *could be* curb numbers.

You could literally go anywhere, to any neighborhood (with a sidewalk) and find work available. But some are better than others. Here are some things to consider:

Volume Potential

What's the biggest factor to keep in mind with curb painting? Volume. That's right. So how does that apply to plotting your course?

There are lots of different types of neighborhoods. Some are based around a 'block' pattern—the streets form a grid. Some are more curvy, with long, swooping streets, short streets, and cul-de-sacs. Some are intermingled with businesses. Some are full of houses with lots of land.

Remember the fact that you're going to be parking your car somewhere ... and walking.

The best neighborhoods for curb painting will be the ones with the most houses in the smallest amount of area. You can only walk so fast, so the more 'crowded-together' the properties are, the better. Grids are great. You can just walk up one side, walk down the other, then move over to the next street and repeat the process. Curvy neighborhoods (prevalent in suburbs) are usually nice too, as long as you have a map with you to keep from getting lost.

"Curb Painting"

It would be best to avoid rural areas, or super-wealthy areas, where you have to walk long distances to get from door to door. Focusing on the volume, remember that you'll want to knock on as many doors as possible in one hour, so the less walking in between the better. Also, you'll want to plan on hitting a whole *chunk* of a neighborhood that's near your car, before moving your car to the next *chunk*. So keeping to tight-knit neighborhoods keeps you from going *too* far from your car, thus minimizing down-time when you're done with an area. Of course, you'll want to plan your route so that you're knocking on doors all the way *back* to your car, too.

Neighborhood Demographics

This has been largely an area of speculation for me, and I haven't been able to really nail down any consistent patterns. It's also a little controversial to stereotype, but I'll put this out there, and you can do with it as you like.

Is there a certain type of neighborhood, or a certain demographic of potential customers that is better than others?

I've of-times looked for neighborhoods that were somewhere within the realm of the middle class. I've experimented with older neighborhoods, new 'cracker-box house' neighborhoods, higher-income neighborhoods, slums—you name it.

"Curb Painting"

There have been times when I thought that neighborhoods full of retired elderly people were more likely to buy my services, since they keep their properties nice and tend to have money to spend. I've had a lot of luck with the elderly—even paying to have their neighbors' curbs done as well. But I've also had a lot of them quick to close the door in my face before they even knew what I was offering. So, no pattern.

I once looked up the average income by zip code in my city, and went to the highest income area that still had normal, tight-knit neighborhoods. These people had money, but I had no more success there, specifically, than other areas. Perhaps the people with more income are more frugal, and more resistant to touching up their curb. Then again, many of them were happy to.

"Curb Painting"

In the beginning, I avoided the really poor, 'slum' neighborhoods, thinking that they wouldn't have the money to spend frivolously on curb painting. Those people surprised me, however, by giving me no difference in results over wealthier neighborhoods. Maybe they're more frivolous with the little money they have, so were less resistant to being sold. Maybe not.

The point here is that, while I tried to pigeonhole different neighborhoods and be able to predict my results by demographic, for one reason or another, I had similar results everywhere. Five bucks is five bucks to anybody, and anywhere you go, you'll find people willing to spend money on this kind of service, and people that aren't.

"Curb Painting"

The only possible demographic that I suppose really makes a difference is a neighborhood with *lots* of *rentals*. If a potential customer is renting their home, you might have a harder time selling your service. Most renters don't make any adjustments (no matter how small) to the property without the permission of the landlord. Of course, some of them will buy your service anyway. So, if you're in a neighborhood and hearing every other person say that they're 'just renting', you might want to move a few blocks down. Don't worry, though—I'll include a script for dealing with renters so that you can still attempt a sale when they sheepishly tell you that it's not their house.

Best Times to Work

Since your income will be extremely reliant upon volume, it will be best to work during the times when people are *at home*. There's no point in focusing so much on volume, knocking on the maximum number of doors possible for the time spent, if no one is around.

The best times to go out curb painting are any time on the weekend (don't start *too* early—people sleep in), and during the late afternoon and evenings during the week. Sure, if you go out at 11am on Tuesday, you'll get *some* people who work from home, are unemployed, retired, or have abnormal working hours, and *of course*, some people work during the evenings and weekends, but ... the majority of Americans are 9-to-5'ers.

"Curb Painting"

The more people that are home, the less doors go unanswered. The more doors are answered, the more potential customers. The more potential customers, the more possible *yes*'s and jobs sold.

National holidays are great, because a lot of people will be off and relaxing (or partying) at home. A bright and sunny Saturday—you know the kind where kids are playing outside and guys are washing their cars—are also nice.

You can still make money during the slow times, but it's harder, and you'll do a lot better if you work yourself around the majority of America's schedule. I usually hit the streets at four or five pm on the weekdays, ten in the morning on Saturdays, and noon or one o'clock on Sundays (to let people come home from church).

Working with the Map

Here's where you can really bump up you volume. Try to become really efficient at using a route to maximize the number of doors knocked, and make sure you're not doubling back anywhere and wasting your time. The best way I've found to tackle a 'chunk' of a neighborhood is to go up one side of a street, then down the other. Deviate onto any side-streets when you find them, up and then back down, but look at the map frequently, and make sure you're not wasting any areas, skipping any sections, and deliberately leave yourself a way back to the car that you didn't already hit. Take a look at some of the diagrams for example:

"Curb Painting"

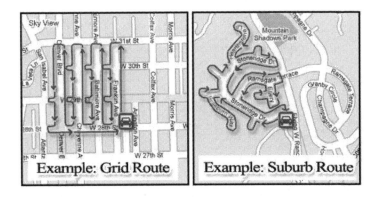

In a *grid* neighborhood, you can decide how many blocks you want to go in one direction (example: a North-South street), go up one side until your chosen turn-around point, then come back down, hitting the connecting (East-West) streets on the return trip. Then, back at the beginning, you can head over to the next (North-South) street, and continue the process. This way, you can hit them all.

Curvy, suburb neighborhoods will take a little more getting used to, since the streets don't

"Curb Painting"

always follow any sort of pattern and can get a little *weird* sometimes, but keeping a route (and using flexible deviations) will become second nature in no time.

After you're done walking an entire *chunk*, take a highlighter to your map, and highlight the streets (or sections of streets) you hit, so that when you move on to the next area, you won't accidentally hit them again.

One last detail about planning your routes, and what to expect from your day—*bathroom breaks*. Something that most people wouldn't count on is that once you park your car, figure out the pattern of your route, and start knocking on doors, is that two or three hours later, you'll have to go to the bathroom. Especially if you're staying properly hydrated. That means that if you're in the middle

"Curb Painting"

of a suburban neighborhood, the only bathroom you're going to find will be if you get back to your car and drive to a gas station. For this reason, you should plan your forays away from your car not to exceed two to three hours. That way, you're starting to feel nature's call when you're making your way *back* to the car. So you finish an area, mark it down in your notebook, drive to that gas station, then proceed on to the next area.

Facing Your Customers

The first time you grab your bucket, leave the familiar comfort of your home, eye the first house on your route, crisply knock on the door, and face a random human being on the other side ... you'll feel a little surge of adrenaline and stumble through your half-memorized script, thinking "I can't believe I'm doing this."

That's how it went for me the very first house I ever knocked on. The very first time I did *anything* door-to-door. The 30-something woman of Indian-decent dressed in a T-shirt and sweats I found on the other side of the door said, "Sure," and handed me five bucks.

Maybe you're not a shy person. Maybe you just don't care about presenting yourself before a total stranger, and will be able to just run with this little cash job without thinking twice. That's great. This'll be a piece of cake for you.

But if you're *not* a 'people person', or if you don't have any experience in sales or face-to-face

"Curb Painting"

customer service, the idea of door-to-door sales may be downright *terrifying*.

Well, worry not, my introverted reader. Any sort of fear or apprehension you have about this part of the job will be desensitized to the point of non-existence after just a few confrontations. Remember—this is just curb painting. You're not selling alarm systems, or roofs, or cable. It's not even a magazine subscription. You are *invisible*. If they want it, they'll buy it. If they don't, you'll give 'em one or two shots to change their mind. If they still don't want your services, you'll cut them loose and move on. Volume, volume, volume.

For anyone who hasn't done door-to-door work before, or even any sort of sales, I'll throw in a few words.

Working Door to Door

What's the name of the game in door-to-door work? You're probably getting the idea by now: *Volume*.

You'll see a lot of doors that don't get answered, because many people either aren't home, they're in the back yard, they never answer their door to people they don't recognize, or they're afraid of 'salesmen'.

When you actually have a person open their door to you, remember—it's no big deal. We've all been conditioned by stories and T.V. to believe that door-to-door salesmen are hideously abused by their customers, who yell and scream at them, sic

"Curb Painting"

their dog on them, point a shotgun in their face, slam the door in their face, etc. ad nauseam.

Well, that's just not the way it is. The people answering the door are people. People just like you. And most normal folks out there are *respectful* of others, or at least shy and non-confrontational.

I have *never* been violently threatened. Being cursed out or anything similarly silly practically *never* happens. You'd be amazed at how rare it is. Perhaps the only time a customer was ever over-the-line rude with me *didn't throw me off at all*, because the guy was a crazy, fat, old man, who was obviously a few screws loose.

If people *truly* don't want to deal with you, they won't open their door. If they're standing in front of you, and they don't want to buy your service, most of the time they'll politely decline, excuse themselves, and shut the door. *Most* people who say 'no' don't even close the door until you *acknowledge* that they're not interested, and then they'll close the door only after you've both said goodbye to each other. The worst that ever happens is merely a '*not interested*' and a door closed while you're still talking. *Big deal*. And that door is *closed*—not slammed.

Here are a few tricks I've learned about going door to door.

For someone to answer the door, they've got to know you're there. Some peoples' doorbells don't work. I've seen a lot of broken doorbells. When I approach a door, I will knock (or ring) ... *twice*. If I see a doorbell right away, I'll use it. Most doorbells you can *hear* through the door or an open window,

"Curb Painting"

at least faintly. When I knock/ring once, I'll wait ten seconds or so, then knock/ring again. If there's no response the second time, I'll move on. If I ring the doorbell the first time, and suspect that the doorbell isn't working (I'll listen for it), I'll wait ten seconds, *as if it worked*, then I'll knock. If I believe the doorbell isn't working, after trying it once, I'll knock a second time, too.

If I see a doorbell with a broken button, I'll just skip it and knock. Sometimes a broken button will make the electrical connection—sometimes not. If I see a house with *two* doorbells (they're out there), I'll ring them *both* simultaneously, since there's no way to know which one is the good one.

If I feel the need to knock instead of ringing the doorbell, for whatever reason, and there is a *screen-door*, I'll *open* the screen-door, knock on the main, wood door, then close the screen-door again. Wooden doors reverberate throughout the house, like they're designed to do. If you only knock on that aluminum screen-door, there's a good chance that if there *is* a person home, they won't hear you. Most people, I've found, leave their screen-doors unlocked, so this isn't a problem.

What about *'no soliciting'* signs? I'll leave that up to you. Some people might have different ideas about such ethics than others. Personally, I ignore those signs. Unless the sign is surrounded by all sorts of *other* signs reinforcing that the person is really, *really* serious about not being disturbed.

A lot of people put up 'no soliciting' signs just to fend off the door-to-door religious missionaries, or vacuum salesmen. I consider curb painting a

"Curb Painting"

valuable, neighborhood service selling something *cheap enough* that it isn't worth passing up the extra business. And I've gotten lots of business from people with 'no soliciting' signs that I would have otherwise missed. If you knock on doors with those signs, you'll occasionally get a customer who'll grumble a little bit and point out the sign, but all you have to do is excuse yourself politely, wish them a nice day, and move on.

The only real risk of ignoring 'no soliciting' signs is if you were running a 'real' business, you'd be concerned with your reputation. People whose 'no soliciting' signs you ignored could call up the Better Business Bureau and file a complaint that you disrespected their privacy, ignored their sign, or some other such thing. Since you're a one-man operation, with the ability to adapt on the fly and change locations like lightning, this isn't a concern.

Unless you take this in a direction I did not, you won't be listed in your local BBB.

One last, little tidbit about door-to-door work: use the sidewalks. Do NOT cut through peoples' lawns or gardens. There's no need to do it, it's really unprofessional, and it's a sure way to have some angry residents on your hands. It won't really cut *that* much time out of your quest for efficiency and volume anyway—you'll do just fine sticking to sidewalks, driveways, walkways, and flagstone paths.

Scripts

If you're new to any sort of sales, you might think that following a script is pretty *lame*, unnatural, and makes you feel like a robot. But

"Curb Painting"

they help. This book is only a *guide*, after all, and you can run your own show, but there *is* a reason successful salesmen use scripts.

They work.

A good script is really something short and sweet you can memorize that will make your sales points heard as quickly and efficiently as possible, before the customer tunes you out and closes the door. If you had to come up with a fresh description for what you do and why you're knocking on someone's door every time you stood in front of a customer, you'd burn out. It's mentally draining create conversation on the fly for hours on end.

With a basic script, you'll be able to rattle something off without thinking about it, which will leave your mind fresh to focus on rebuttals (retorts), volume, or whatever else you want to think about to pass the time. The key with a script is to know what you're doing well enough to be flexible and quick on your feet, and to be able to speak *naturally*. Without sounding like you're reciting a script. This can be done with practice in front of a mirror, but you'll get better at it the more you do it out in the field.

Here's the basic script, your general pitch, which you'll say to most people:

> **"Hi there. I'm going through your neighborhood today putting everybody's address numbers out on the curb.**
>
> (Motion to where their current curb number is.)

"Curb Painting"

I see yours is pretty faded. Can I touch it up for you for five bucks?"

That's the script you'll say most of the time. As you walk from house to house, make sure to scope out the sidewalk on your way to the *next* house, so that you are familiar with the curb number they already have. This way, you can amend the 'I see yours is pretty faded' with something more specific, if needed. For instance, if their curb number is fairly fresh, say "I see yours is a *little* faded" or "I see yours is a little scuffed up", depending. They're never perfect. The last thing you want to do is say it's 'pretty faded', and hear the customer say, "What? I had it done a month ago! It's fine!" On the other end of the spectrum, it could be *so faded* that it's hardly noticeable. You could amend it with '*really* faded', along with a raise of the eyebrows for effect.

If a house doesn't *have* a curb number at all (be careful, it could be just really, *really* faded), try this one:

> **"Hi there. I'm going through your neighborhood today putting everybody's address numbers out on the curb.**
>
> (Motion to where their current curb number should be.)
>
> **Can I paint yours for you for five bucks?"**

Sometimes, in either cases, you'll get someone who says, "Sure," and comes up with the cash. Most of the time they'll say, "No," or "Not

"Curb Painting"

interested," or utter some lame excuse. In this case, you'll come right back at them with a simple rebuttal. I'll give you some rebuttals in a minute. If they say no *again*, give them a second rebuttal. If they still say no, tell them, "Okay—have a nice day," and move on.

Some of you that are really into sales or arguing might want to go back and forth for a while. Hardcore salesmen follow the adage that, "until they close the door, '*no*' simply means that they need more information to close the sale." Just remember what your focus is. Volume. Don't give them any more than two (quick) rebuttals, then move on and focus on the volume. No point trying to convince a sale out of a customer who might just be a little starved for attention, when you could have hit two more houses in the meantime.

So what happens when they say, "Sure"? Get the money *upfront*, as gently as possible. This isn't a big job, and you certainly won't want to bother wasting time going back to the door when you're done, leading the customer to the sidewalk, waiting for them to approve your work, blah blah blah ... time's-a-wasting.

Once the money is in your hand, say, "Thanks! Have a nice day," then get to work.

If they don't immediately reach for five dollars after agreeing to your service, just linger for a second. That might do it. Or, if they stare at you, unsure of what happens next, you can gently remind them, "It'll be five dollars." Then, they'll say, "Oh—okay," and go off to their wallet, or they'll say, "Oh—you want it now?" In the latter case, you can clear things up by saying something

"Curb Painting"

like, "Yeah, that way I don't have to bother you and come back to the door."

If the customer insists on paying you *after* the curb numbers are complete, *don't argue*. If you argue after they've made up their mind about not paying upfront, you will lose them. Just say, "Okay, I'll be back when I'm done." Paint the numbers. Make sure to do a good job (you're *always* doing a good job, right?), then return to the door. Take the money, thank them, wish them a good day, then move on.

When you're in the unlikely event of waiting for the customer to pay you *after* the job is done, and if you're unlucky enough to have the customer dislike your work or refuse to pay you, don't make a big deal out of it. If there's something that can be fixed, talk about it with the customer and fix it. If there's no way that they'll pay you, for whatever reason, don't get yourself too upset. Swallow the loss, leave the anger behind, and move on. Just so you know, this has *never* happened to me. Once, on a windy day when I was still inexperienced, I had a customer who wanted to pay *after*. My numbers weren't very neat because of the wind and my lack of skill. He pointed it out, I fixed it, then he paid me. I've never been totally snubbed.

Okay. Now for some rebuttals:

"It'll make your house easier to find for the pizza guy..."

> This is usually my first retort. The 'pizza guy' is pretty universal, because most people order delivery food of some sort sometimes, and even if they don't eat pizza,

the customer will automatically realize that 'pizza guy' is replaceable with whatever food they *do* order.

"It'll make your address more visible and easier to find at night…"

This is interchangeable with the 'pizza guy' rebuttal, and is more useful in 'virgin' neighborhoods with no curb numbers, or on a house that doesn't have a porch light, a self-lighting address number on the wall, or bushes covering up the normal address numbers.

"It's only five bucks…"

This is usually my second rebuttal. It's not terribly useful, because by the time I use it, the customer's mind is already closed, but it has won them over once and a while.

If they say, **"Can you come back on (whatever day)?"**

Say, **"Well, I'm just passing through *this* neighborhood *today*. I've done lots of your neighbors, and it's just five bucks..."**

If they say, **"I don't have five bucks,"** or, **"I don't have any cash."**

If you feel that they're otherwise pretty warm to the sale, you could try, **"That's okay—I can take a check, or ... do you just not quite have *five* dollars?"** If they feel like writing a check, fine. If they don't have *five* dollars, but they have *three*, feel free to

"Curb Painting"

> work for a lower rate in this circumstance if it's okay with you.

If they say, **"Five bucks?! I won't pay you five bucks just for some numbers!"**

> Say, **"Well, your numbers *are* really faded. I've touched up a lot of houses here, and it'll last for over a year! It's *just* five bucks..."** Or, feel free to negotiate a lower rate if you like.

Earlier in this book, I mentioned that it's a good idea to always start your day with $15 in change in your pocket. You will come across people who only have a ten, or only have a twenty. If you neglect to start with any change, however, or have changed a lot of people out during the day and at some point only have tens and twenties yourself, try this:

"Curb Painting"

"I only have a ten / twenty. Do you have change?"

Rummage your hand through your pocket, or quickly look over your change. **"Um, no—sorry. I don't have change. (I only have twenties.)"**

If they have a ten:
"Tell you what, do you have a neighbor you'd like me to do? I can do yours *and* theirs for your ten…"

If they have a twenty:
"Tell you what, I can do some of you neighbors for you, too. In fact, I'll give you five for the price of four. I'll do yours and four of your

"Curb Painting"

> neighbors. Which ones are your friends?"

If they say, **"Sorry—we're renting."**

> Say, **"I gotcha. Well, I've never seen a landlord turn down this sort of thing. It'll make the address more visible, and it's only five bucks..."**

> Or, **"I gotcha. Well, I've never seen any problems with that. Technically, the curb isn't part of the property. It's something that will help *you*. And it's only five bucks..."**

All of these scripts and rebuttals are the basic foundation of what to say to your customers. You could get by and have a perfectly profitable curb painting cash job by simply memorizing them, and being able to rattle them off word-for-word. As you get into the job, however, you might find yourself personalizing them. Changing them here and there to suit your personality, or to adjust for your environment. This is fine. The key is to remember that you should be reciting your scripts *fluidly*. Make sure that whatever you say sounds natural—like talking in a normal conversation. The better you are with sales and talking to people, the warmer you'll be able to make these scripts, and the more you'll be able to adapt to whatever the customer says in order to respond with exactly what they need to hear to buy your service and hand over five dollars.

However you adjust the scripts, or write new scripts, to suit your needs, keep them short and simple. Customers will only hear you if you get to the point right away.

<u>Painting That Curb</u>

So, you've talked with the customer, maybe thrown a rebuttal or two at them, and now you have five bucks more to your name than you did a minute ago. Time to get to work.

Once you get the process down, painting the curb is really easy, and should take you two to five minutes if you try to do it efficiently and don't waste any time. After a quick paint-job, you're moving on. With the time it takes to actually paint a curb, if you somehow sold job after job (*'yes'* after *'yes'*) with no time wasted in between, the most I'd say you can do in an hour (MAX) is 10-12 jobs. That would be a legendary string of sales (or a single customer paying for all his neighbors), but with all the stars and planets in alignment, and everyone home and in a super-good mood, $50-$60 per hour would be the most you could make at five dollars a job.

A word on spray paint cans, in case you've never touched one before in your life. When you have a fresh can, you'll have to start it off by shaking it vigorously for a good 30 seconds. There's a little marble in there (that's what makes that the 'shaking' sound) mixing up all the paint. When the shaking is finished and you're ready to paint, *ALWAYS*, when you put your finger on the 'trigger', check to make sure which direction the nozzle is pointing before you fire. Make it a habit to check the direction of the spray, and make sure your finger in on the right spot *before* you initiate

"Curb Painting"

spraying. If you become lazy, and try to line up the can by feel, you'll only have to spray yourself in the face *once* before you decide never to spray without checking again. (Just so you know, I've never shot myself in the face—I just know the importance of such safety.) Also, with spray paint, when you're finished for the day, you'll want to clear the paint out of the nozzle and lines before driving home. Otherwise, the paint can dry up *inside* the nozzle, and create a permanent blockage, ruining the rest of the can. Clear the lines by holding the can *upside down* and spraying it until only air (no paint) comes from the nozzle. You'll also know the nozzle is clear because of the sound—it'll *hiss* instead of sizzle and spit.

You'll most likely be painting right over the old, faded curb numbers that were already there. If it's so faded that it's practically invisible, you could, at your option, treat it as if there is no curb address at all, or suggest a better location to the customer. If there is *no* curb address, go ahead and choose the best position for the new one yourself, or feel free to ask the customer (and suggest locations for him) if he's still hanging around outside or by the door. If there is a vehicle parked in the way of the old curb number (which you'll be retouching), or the position for the new one, inform the customer and see if he'll either move the vehicle, or allow you to paint in another location.

The best location for a curb address, if you're choosing a new location or painting numbers in front of a house that hasn't had them before, is about a foot off of the edge of the driveway, on whichever side looks better and seems more centered over the property. Don't paint *too close* to the driveway, or the numbers will be run over

"Curb Painting"

(and smudged with tire-black) whenever someone pulls in or out of the drive an angle. If the customer is out there with you, asking him his opinion and making suggestions isn't necessary, but it will increase their customer service experience.

Some pre-existing curb numbers may be different than others. The great majority of curb numbers will be a white field background with black blocky, universal numbers, the same size and otherwise identical to the ones you'll be painting. Most curb numbers will only be on the vertical side of the curb. In the case of a sloped curb, it'll be the same, only following the angle of the curb.

Here are some *other* types of curb numbers you may encounter:

Double

Some houses with a vertical curb will have a *double* set of the curb numbers—one on the vertical side, and one on the flat side, their white backgrounds connected. These can be an annoyance, because it'll take you twice as long to paint. Unless the customer specifically instructs me to touch up both sides, if the top is at least *moderately* okay, I'll just touch up the bottom (vertical) number and move on.

Reverse Color

Some rare curb numbers will be white numbers on a black background (reversed colors). If a reverse number is *very* faded, just paint over it with normal colors (white background, black numbers). If the black background is still strong enough to show

"Curb Painting"

through a new, white background, paint it with the reverse colors. I try to avoid painting reverse colors whenever possible, because I always carry less black in my kit than white.

Flag

Occasionally, especially with elderly or retired veteran customers, you'll see a standard curb number, but with a picture of a US Flag on one side of the white background. When you paint over it, protect the flag section, so there will still be a flag next to the new, white background. Don't paint over someone's flag.

Step One: Prep Work

Set your kit down next to where you'll be painting. Make sure you can see the address number of the house—either if it's on the wall of the house next to the door, on the mailbox, or on the old curb number. If there is any debris in the gutter where you'll be painting, clear it out before you sit down. Use your shoes, your wire brush, or your gloved hand. Make sure that there is no dirt caked on the specific area you're about to paint—wipe or brush it off.

Take out your placemat, gardening mat, or whatever you bought to sit on, and have a seat. Or just sit down on the road. Pull out the stencils you'll need, and set them down in a way that won't let them blow away in the wind. Pull out your white paint, black paint, and shake them if you

"Curb Painting"

need to (if it hasn't been done in a while). Keep your dustpan nearby.

Step Two: The First Layer

Before you start painting, make sure you're *absolutely certain* of the address number. You don't want to paint the wrong number.

To begin, line up your paint shield over the existing white background. Try to keep it centered over the old one, so that the new numbers will mostly line up with and cover the old numbers. If you're painting a *vertical* curb number, the folded section of the paint shield should sit on the ground at just the right height. The fold is a guide, however, so if it doesn't line up, it's no big deal—just line the shield up however you need. On a sloped curb, the folded section won't come into play at all.

Hold the paint shield tight against the curb. I use my feet, one foot on either side, to keep the shield taut and flush against the curb. (Of course, you've got to wear shoes that you don't mind *painting* a little.)

Paint the white background.

In case you haven't spray-painted anything before, make sure you really take it easy on the 'flow'. As you spray, the nozzle should be 4-6 inches away from the curb. And instead of holding the trigger down, just spray in short, controlled spurts. Don't let the paint get heavy *anywhere*. We're talking a very *light* layer—the minimum you need to get the color you want. Any heavier than that, and it'll take forever to dry and the paint might *run*. Use as little paint as possible, make sure your edges are good to go, and make sure the color is even over the entire rectangular, white background.

When you feel the background is complete, carefully remove the paint shield and set it aside. (Make sure it won't blow away.)

Step Three: Between Layers

Take your dustpan, if you elected to bring one along, and fan your white background for sixty seconds or so. If you didn't bring a dustpan ... wait. The concrete will absorb the paint pretty quickly, and it'll dry rapidly, as long as you didn't paint it too heavy. When the background is no longer

"Curb Painting"

glistening, you can use your stencils for the next phase without them sticking to the curb.

Step Four: The Second Layer

Double check the address number on the house again, and shake your black paint.

If you have normal stencils:

>Arrange the stencils on the white background, side-by-side, centered horizontally so the numbers will be in the middle of the background. Be gentle, so you don't disrupt your white background. If there are two of the same number (example: the address is 2661), arrange the numbers you *have*, and center the entire

"Curb Painting"

arrangement by visualizing where you imagine the finished number will be.

Holding down the edges of each stencil with the gloved fingers of one hand (or your putty knife), carefully and *lightly* spray the number with your black paint in short, tiny bursts, until you have an even amount of black over the entire number and the edges are clear. Be careful not to let your spray go around the edges of the stencil (difficult with standard stencils). Be *especially* careful not to spray to heavily anywhere, because the numbers are what tend to run, and it'll look horrible if your numbers are 'bleeding' onto your white background.

When you've finished the first number, carefully remove it and set it aside. Move on to the next number. With the stencils side-by-side, the numbers will have the perfect amount of space between each other.

When all of the numbers are complete, the stencils should be laying on the street next to you, and you should have a pristine, new curb number with no runs, and no sparse patches in the paint. At this point you'll move on, and in twenty minutes or so, the number you just painted will be dry and looking great.

If you made some of my custom **'divider' stencils**:

Set the stencils you'll need next to you on the street. You can leave the rest in the bucket. Since you can't line up the numbers,

"Curb Painting"

you'll have to be a little better at visualizing the width of the entire address number, and figuring out where you'll have to put your numbers to have the whole thing centered in the white background. If this seems challenging, don't worry—you'll have it down soon enough.

Remember the black box you traced on the dividers with marker at the edge of the original stencils when you created your 'divider' stencils? It'll come in handy now. The semi-transparency of the dividers will let you see the background beneath, and as you paint each number, you'll be able to see them through the next stencil, allowing you to line up each number with the last, and with the right amount of space in between.

Place the first stencil over the white background, after you visualize the entire address number and figure out where the first individual number should be. Hold the stencil down so that the number is tight against the curb. Spray the number *lightly*, just like I discussed above. When finished, carefully remove the stencil, and put it back in your bucket (unless you'll need the same number again).

Take the next stencil and put it against the curb (gently—don't smear the number you just painted). You should be able to see the number you just painted *through* the semi-transparent stencil, and can line up the 'box' of the stencil with the imagined 'box' of the last number.

"Curb Painting"

Repeat until finished. Using the custom divider stencils is quicker, less messy, and virtually *eliminates* the over-spray which is so difficult to avoid with the standard stencils.

After you paint your numbers, there's no need to fan them with the dustpan—you're done. The whole process should take no longer than five minutes. Pick up your kit, replace everything in the bucket, and move on to the next house.

Recording Your Results

So you're in this little cash business to make money, right? And you're making the most money

"Curb Painting"

you can by focusing on Volume, Income per Hour, and Quality, right?

Well, how are you going to know you're results—how much you're making, what's working better for you, and what's not working so well ... unless you write it all down?

If you're just trying to make a quick buck, sure—you don't need to bother with records. But if you're trying to approach this like a professional, like a businessman, and you're going to be painting curbs for more than just a single, experimental *day*, you'll want to keep track of your results.

Keep a notebook and some pens/pencils in the car, or in a backpack, if you're carrying one. You'll be writing something in your notebook every time

"Curb Painting"

you finish a 'chunk' of a neighborhood, and figuring it all out at the end of the day.

If you want to keep track of *everything*, start your curb painting notebook with a page listing all the initial supplies you purchased, their cost, and the total monetary amount of your initial investment. This way, you'll know how much you have to earn before you're in profit-mode—after your initial investment is re-made.

Each day curb painting, you'll be keeping track of the following:

- Each 2-3 hour block (the amount of time spent in one small area, in between moving your car to another area, breaks, etc.), separated, including:
    - The date

"Curb Painting"

- The time you start and finish a neighborhood 'chunk'
- The neighborhood area, with Map References (page number, grid number, etc.) to help you look up the area again
- Notes about the neighborhood
- Total time for the day
- Total money made for the day
- Hourly income for the day—Figure your hourly income based on money made divided by time worked

"Curb Painting"

> **Saturday, 23 May 2009**
>
> 10:00am - 11:30am $30   pg.893 A2 (Sam Jonas)
> 11:45am - 1:45pm $40   pg.893 A2
> 2:30pm - 4:45pm $35   pg.893 A3
>   - Lots of security doors and fences, hard access
> 5:00pm - 6:00pm $15   pg.893 A3
>   - Some rentals
>
> Total Time 1:30 + 2 + 2:15 + 1 = 5:45
> Total Income   = $120
>   ~ $21 per hour

If you choose to be completely thorough, include any expenses: the original expenses and any other expenses you incur, from replenishing your paint, perhaps gas, and include them in your daily results. That way, you can keep track over your total income (gross), as well as your income adjusted *after* you factor in and subtract the expenses (net). You could even go one step further, and figure your hourly income based on your net (after expenses are deducted), instead of basing it off of your gross (like above), to give you a more accurate look at how much money you're making, and what your time spent is earning for you.

Constantly figuring your hourly income is a good way to put the whole business in perspective. You might be able to determine patterns that lead to higher income at certain times or in certain areas than others. Looking at your notes about your work and the neighborhoods you worked in might give you clues about ways to *increase* that income. Figuring out your average hourly income will also let you make plans and goals, depending on how much money you want to earn. If you know you make an average of $15 per hour, and you need to come up with an extra $300 a week (for whatever your reasons), you'll know you have to work that curb painting *cash job* for 20 hours a

"Curb Painting"

week—perhaps two evenings, and a good-sized day on Saturday and Sunday.

Keeping notes on your neighborhoods will tell you which neighborhoods to continue working the next day, or if you may as well move on to another area of town. Notes could tell you that you're hitting mostly *rentals*, or having to waste a lot of time walking across business fronts. Or any number of things. Keep short notes about your work, and looking back on such notes will help you plan and strategize for better profits in the future.

What Others Have Done

Here are some final ideas on curb painting—ideas that I've considered but never implemented, or things I've seen other curb painters do:

Returning to an Already-Worked Neighborhood

Sometimes you might walk a whole section of a neighborhood, and feel like nearly every house you've knocked on has been unattended. No one is home. Bad timing, coincidence—whatever—you may be thinking about going back to give it another run. You may be considering hitting that section again even if you *did* have plenty of customers home, just to give the ones you already saw another chance, perhaps get an opportunity to talk to someone else, and hit the 'not home's.

"Curb Painting"

If I actually go through a section and 95% of the potential customers are not home, I *might* go back, but that's a pretty big *might*. This is a volume business. Going over an area again, where I've already heard a lot of *no*'s will waste a lot of time, because the people that say *no* will most-certainly say *no* again. And since you're not using any sort of 'print-out' with everyone's names and addresses to guide you, there's no way to remember who was home before, who rejected your service, and who said *yes*.

Hitting the same spot twice is not recommended. Whatever your theories or ideas may suggest, returning to an area will simply take away from your numbers. Just keep moving on to other neighborhoods. There are *many*. Many, many. If you're highlighting the streets in your map as you complete them, you'll know the areas you've hit, and the areas where you have not yet been. Fill up that map-book with highlighted streets. If you ever manage to complete your entire town/city (that's not going to happen, but *if*), buy another map-book, or a different color highlighter, and start over again at the beginning. If you systematically made your way through town the first time, it will have been *several months* since you were in your first neighborhood last.

Pre-canvassing

Something that I've seen other curb painters do is 'pre-canvass' a neighborhood. If you want to try it, this means that you'll do some marketing in a neighborhood intended for curb painting, *before* the curb painting itself actually takes place:

"Curb Painting"

To pre-canvass, you'll go through a neighborhood, on foot (just like curb painting but without your kit), house to house, section by section, putting *flyers* on peoples' doors, on main intersections, communal mail-boxes, and wherever else you think the neighborhood's residents might be. The flyers, which you'll make on your computer, announce that on such-and-such a date (probably one day on the weekend), you'll be passing through their neighborhood painting address numbers out on the curb. They'll go on to say that if that particular resident would like to partake in your services, they can leave five dollars under their doormat by 10am (or something like that).

"Curb Painting"

On the day advertised in the flyer, you'll return with your curb painting kit, and go door to door collecting money from doormats and painting curbs with *little to no* interaction with the customers.

There are several problems with this approach.

"Curb Painting"

First of all, most people don't ever bother to *read* flyers put on their doors. *Many* companies advertise with door flyers (sandwich shops, roofing companies, cable companies, Chinese restaurants, pizza joints, etc.), so a lot of people just rip them off as soon as they notice them and throw them away—perhaps after some angry crumpling action and a few curses.

There's also no guarantee that your flyer will be intercepted by the home-owner. Kids can grab them before their parents have a chance to see them, and either throw them away or lose them before passing them on. Teenagers or other adults in the house might toss them before giving the home-owner a chance to see the flyer, based on the assumption that the home-owner simply wouldn't be interested.

"Curb Painting"

Next point: flyers can't retort. You'll have *no rebuttals*. The only customers you'll get with flyers are the ones that would have given you a simple, "Okay, sure," in the first place. Most of your sales will come after the customer overcomes the initial fear of a salesman at their door, and you've given them one or two quick rebuttals. On top of that, most of those 'easy' customers are buying your service on *impulse*. With a flyer acting as your salesman, there will be *plenty* of time for them to change their minds, or be dissuaded by someone else in their house.

Flyers also cost money. Even if you're making small flyers that print four-to-a-page, you'll have to pay for the printing (or copying) and tape (for attaching them to doors) at the least. It's not much, more it's more that *zero*.

"Curb Painting"

And then there's the obvious: it'll take *twice* as long to work any particular neighborhood. If you canvass it, then paint it, you'd be walking the same neighborhood twice. Since the canvassing pass will be *pro-bono*, you'll cut your income from game day in half.

I haven't done any pre-canvassing, for all of those reasons, because five bucks a pop is too small to invest any time in marketing. Besides— more bad things can happen with such an approach. Hell, there might be a clever (but unethical) kid in the neighborhood who knows that a lot of people are going to be putting a fiver under their doormats on Saturday, and he'll go collecting before you paint your way through...

Appointments

Another idea I've seen suggested, but never put into use, was that of making appointments with potential customers. There are a few ways to do that:

1. You could essentially pre-canvass the neighborhood, but instead of passing out flyers (or in *addition* to passing out flyers), you could knock on doors and make appointments with homeowners for curb painting on a particular future date.

2. You could treat this cash job like many other higher-paying client-based service jobs, advertise with your name and number, and let customers make appointments with you over the phone,

"Curb Painting"

>your website, etc., to have you paint their curb on a future date.

I think going door-to-door to make appointments is silly, when you could just be painting their curb *on the spot*. If you take the time to walk a whole neighborhood, setting up appointments with customers (who are home) for *a* future date, there's no reason why you shouldn't be carrying your kit and painting that curb *right then*, instead of later. Returning later is just a waste of time.

When you're curb painting, you may, rarely, come across a customer who would rather you come back on a certain day. Likewise, if you were advertising in any way that encourages customers to call you and make an appointment, you may have several different appointments for curb painting all over town.

One appointment for a five dollar touch-up is not worth the drive. It'll cost you five dollars for the amount of paint you use and the gas to drive there and back. In the case of the rare customer in the last paragraph, I reply that I'm only passing through their neighborhood just that one time, and move to sell them right away. Any other form of appointment setting that isn't limited to a *single* neighborhood on a *specific* day at a *specific* time is folly. You've got to make enough income to make it worth your time.

Other Paint Shields and Stencils

Like I said earlier in this book, it is *hard* to find equipment specifically designed for curb painting. That said, such equipment *is* out there.

I've seen other curb painters (on the internet) who have paint shields that look like a picture box (a three-dimensional box sized for the white background and eliminating all over-spray), as well as stencils that clip, slide, or otherwise attach together. Of course, in the quest for efficiency, you could always design and create better gear.

A 'picture box' paint shield, for instance, wouldn't be hard to make—but it would still have its limitations. If you built a box out of 1x6's, kind of like a flower-box without a bottom, you could just lay it up against the curb and spray. But ... a paint shield made of non-flexible material (like wood) wouldn't be able to hug a curved curb, or achieve good edges on a sloped curb. And a picture-box paint shield would be heavy to carry around all day.

The few stencils I've come across on the internet that weren't the cheap, universal 'Lowes' types were *ridiculously* expensive. I'm talking $100 plus. My sensibilities never allowed me to look too closely at such over-priced products, but if you *really* wanted some of those fancy, interlocking stencils, you'd probably have to pay dearly for them.

In the beginning of my curb painting days, I was always trying to come up with ideas for better stencils, better paint shields, better kits overall, sketching up designs for locking stencils with built-

"Curb Painting"

in shields and so on, but, *ultimately*, the kit I've covered in this book is the most cost-effective and efficient way to go.

Chapter 4: Summary

So you're interested in making some extra cash on the side?

Well, as you've read in this book, curb painting is definitely a way to make extra cash—whether you're desperately trying to make ends meet, tired of searching for a lousy, low-paying job, just trying to save up some extra money for something you want, or supplementing the income from your day-job.

If you *haven't* read this book, and are the sort of person who just skips to the summary ... *go back and read it*, you lazy oaf! It's a very short book—a 'little book of extra cash'. I'll touch back on the

"Curb Painting"

basic points again here, but there's a lot to learn in the meat of the other three chapters.

In the beginning, you can buy the entire kit, options and all, if you like. But, you may not have much money right now, for whatever reason. You don't have to buy *everything*. You could start out with the most basic of basics, the minimum amount of paint, no change in your pockets, and hit the streets, returning to buy more supplies after you've made some money. As I said in Chapter 2, you could start this little cash job with no more than *twenty bucks*. And if you go whole-hog and buy everything you may *ever* need, you still won't spend more than $50 or so.

The **minimum** you'll need is:
- Stencils
- A Bucket

"Curb Painting"

- Poster Board (for the Paint Shield)
- Gloves
- One can of black spray paint
- Two cans of white spray paint
- Water

Other things that will better your business, in order of importance:

- More paint
- A City Map, or Map-book (better)
- Highlighter
- Notebook and Pens / Pencils
- Something to Sit / Kneel on
- A Dustpan
- Painting masks
- Wire Brush
- Putty knife
- Better stencils

"Curb Painting"

Once your 'kit' is assembled, it's time to pound the pavement. The job is really easy, compared to most jobs. It simply comes down to walking, following a script, painting, and collecting five-dollar bills.

Remember: Focus on the *volume*. That's what's going to keep you moving forward. That's what's going to bump up the hourly income. That's what's going to keep you whistling and bouncing in your steps from door to door, especially when you feel like you've been facing a lot of rejection. Any door-to-door work is a *numbers* game, curb painting more than most. The product/service you're offering in curb painting is so small, all those '*no*'s you'll encounter won't matter at all. Focus on the volume. Knocking on as many doors and putting

"Curb Painting"

yourself in front of as many potential customers as you can is your primary goal.

Set your monetary goals and mark your progress with 'income per hour'. Keep track of the time, and watch your sales, hour by hour. Two sales in an hour is $10/hour. Three is $15. Four is $20. Simple and effective. Work toward goals of however much you want to make, per hour, focus on the volume (which will take you there), and the time will *fly by* as five-dollar bills accumulate in your pocket.

And don't forget to do a good job. You're offering a very easy service, and making decent money for doing so. Make sure the customer gets the best curb numbers their money can buy. This isn't a book about the ethics of Capitalism, but you can take pride in your work, and take comfort in

"Curb Painting"

your ability to go out on your own two feet and make a living out of thin air. For the time being, we still live in a Capitalist economic system, and *that* is the *best* economic system in the history of the world. Any man (or woman) can apply their mind, creativity, and hard work, and create whatever sort of life for themselves they choose. In learning little extra cash jobs like these, you are learning 'an extra way to fish', so to speak, and will always have something to fall back on when your normal income isn't good enough..

Once you're out there in the field, you'll maximize your volume and efficiency (read: profit) if you learn to make the best out of using your map (carry it with you) to create a *route* for each section of neighborhood. That means always thinking ahead, planning which streets you're going to hit, and making sure you hit *every house* on each side of the street, which no time spent doubling back over an area you already passed through. You should be knocking on doors from the moment you step out of the car to when you get back inside.

While you're going door-to-door, you're going to encounter a lot of people who aren't home (more people are home on the weekends and in the evenings), and you'll see a lot of people who aren't interested. Every time someone rejects your offer, you're getting closer and closer to the person who'll say *'yes'*. So, don't take the rejection personally—it's a *numbers* game. And when someone *does* say *'no'*, throw a rebuttal or two at them. The quick, simple rebuttals in the Chapter 3 will turn enough rejections into sales that it would be foolish to just accept every *'no'* and move on. Many potential customers will say *'no'* without even knowing or fully understanding what you're

"Curb Painting"

offering, because they're afraid of being taken advantage of.

On the other hand, don't get so into the sales aspect of curb painting that you're spending a lot of time trying to convince the customer to give you five bucks. Shoot 'em two rebuttals, then cut them loose and move on. Remember, it's about the volume.

Get the money *upfront*. This way, you can just wish the customer a good day, do your work, and move on immediately. If the customer is too weird about or adamantly against paying upfront, don't sweat it. If you press them too hard, you'll drive them off, and lose the sale. Smile, do the job, and return for the money.

"Curb Painting"

When you're painting the curb, spray the paint *very lightly*. Light, short spurts. It's really easy to lay it on too thick, and then, you'll be waiting for it to dry, or worse, your paint will *run*. Focus on painting *evenly*, just enough to get the full color (white or black) over the entire area. And before you start painting the numbers, double-check the address number by looking at the wall of the house or the mailbox.

At the end of every 'chunk' of a neighborhood, when you get back to your car, record your time (round to the nearest 'fifteen minutes'), your income, details about where you were on the map, and any notes about the neighborhood, thoughts about your work, etc.

At the end of the day, add it all up and figure your hourly rate. Subtract expenses (if you want to

"Curb Painting"

be thorough), and you'll have your net income for the day.

The best part about curb painting as a little cash job is that it's easy, anyone who can walk can do it, and you don't need much to get started. So, now that you've read through this book in its entirety, go ahead and scrape up whatever you need to buy your initial supplies, make your paint shield (and maybe some better stencils), and …

GET TO WORK!

I hope you enjoyed this 'little book of extra cash', and I hope it helps you to bring some extra income to your life. Be sure to keep up with the other *Little Books of Extra Cash* for more ideas on working with creativity, innovation, and some good, old-fashioned, American 'get up and go'.

Please take the time to leave a review on Amazon. It goes a *long* way to making this book (and my other books) more visible.

Please leave a review for this book on Amazon! You'll find it at:

amazon.com/author/eddiepatin

Be prosperous…

"Curb Painting"

Please sign up for my MAILING LIST to receive occasional news about new titles!

www.LostWoodsPublishing.com/eddiepatin

About the Author - Eddie Patin

Author, entrepreneur, adventurer. Born in south Louisiana, Eddie Patin has lived the majority of his life in beautiful Colorado, USA.

A business owner and consultant during the day, Eddie spends his nights and weekends building a career as a writer, an artist, and a musician. He is passionate about his music (under the band name,

"Curb Painting"

"Fire and Stone"), the pursuit of excellence in firearms, combat arts, and medieval weaponry, and is a proponent of Capitalism and the Free Market.

His favorite authors are Ayn Rand and Stephen King, and his favorite fiction genres are fantasy, science fiction, and horror. In his book catalog, you'll find a combination of grim fiction, business non-fiction, and children's books.

Visit Eddie Patin's Author Page on Amazon.com!
http://www.Amazon.com/author/eddiepatin

His titles can be found at Lost Woods Publishing LLC:
http://LostWoodsPublishing.com

Please join Eddie Patin's MAILING LIST to receive occasional updated about new titles.
http://LostWoodsPublishing.com/eddiepatin

More Titles from Eddie Patin

And Other Non-Fiction Authors from Lost Woods Publishing LLC

Eddie Patin – Fiction Books

In Darkness of Mountain's Night – A Hunter's Tale (Dark Fantasy Horror)

"Curb Painting"

Reclaiming the Maze

(A Fantasy Story about a Minotaur)

Forgotten Tales from the Realms of Primoria

Hijacked on Naos 5

The Chronicles of Alex Varia

Science Fiction from the Primoria Universe

"Curb Painting"

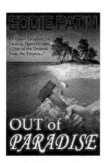

Out of Paradise

(Medieval Zombie Fantasy Fiction from the Tropics)

Forgotten Tales from the Realms of Primoria

"Curb Painting"

Eddie Patin – Non-Fiction Books

Curb Painting for Spare Income – How to Guide

Make Side Cash by Painting Curb Numbers from the

"Little Books of Extra Cash" Series

Oren Suzuki – "Organized for Life" Series

The famous author of "DeClutter Magic" presents the home organization system designed from lessons from his Japanese grandmother.

DeClutter Magic – Tips for Organizing, Simplifying, and Tidying your Home from my Japanese Grandmother

DeClutter Magic 2 – The Three Essential Questions for Decluttering, Organizing, and Tidying Up your Home

"Curb Painting"

You'll find Oren Suzuki here:

Amazon.com/author/orensuzuki

A Message from Lost Woods Publishing

If you enjoyed this book and would like to hear about new titles from Eddie Patin, we'd like to invite you to sign up for free updates of new titles (no spam, we promise!) by visiting:

http://LostWoodsPublishing.com/eddiepatin

In fact, we care so much about keeping our regular readers happy, every month we are offering a free drawing for an Amazon Gift Card in exchange for signing up for our newsletter!

"Curb Painting"

Be sure to visit the main publishing website from time to time to see our new books from other authors as well, and feel free to sign up for our newsletter to receive free updates.

Again, we thank you sincerely for purchasing this book and supporting the author.

http://LostWoodsPublishing.com

Made in the USA
Middletown, DE
07 December 2018